SAVE EARTH'S ANIMALS!

Endangered Animals of AUSTRALIA

Marie Allgor

PowerKiDS press™

New York

Published in 2011 by The Rosen Publishing Group, Inc.
29 East 21st Street, New York, NY 10010

First Edition

Editor: Jennifer Way
Book Design: Julio Gil

Photo Credits: Cover © Cyril Ruoso/Peter Arnold, Inc.; p. 4 Tom Brakefield/Stockbyte/Thinkstock; pp. 5 (top), 7 (bottom) Hemera/Thinkstock; p. 5 (bottom) Comstock/Thinkstock; pp. 6, 7, 12 Jupiterimages/Photos.com/Thinkstock; pp. 7 (top), 8, 9, 10, 16 iStockphoto/Thinkstock; p. 11 Stanley Breeden/National Geographic/Getty Images; pp. 13, 14–15 Bert and Babs Wells/Getty Images; pp. 17, 19, 20, 21, 22 Shutterstock.com; p. 18 Jason Edwards/Getty Images.

Library of Congress Cataloging-in-Publication Data

Allgor, Marie.
  Endangered animals of Australia / by Marie Allgor. — 1st ed.
      p. cm. — (Save earth's animals!)
  Includes index.
  ISBN 978-1-4488-2530-1 (library binding) — ISBN 978-1-4488-2644-5 (pbk.) —
ISBN 978-1-4488-2645-2 (6-pack)
  1. Endangered species—Australia—Juvenile literature. 2. Wildlife conservation—Australia—Juvenile literature. I. Title.
  QL84.7.A1A45 2011
  591.680994—dc22
                                                    2010022494

Manufactured in the United States of America

CPSIA Compliance Information: Batch #WW11PK: For Further Information contact Rosen Publishing, New York, New York at 1-800-237-9932

Contents

Welcome to Australia!

Australia is one of Earth's seven continents. Australia is both a country and a continent! Australia is also an island.

Many of Australia's animals are **marsupials**, such as the kangaroo. **Indigenous** Australians have lived on the continent for thousands of years. When Europeans began to settle in Australia in the 1700s, they brought their farm animals and pets.

The kangaroo is one of Australia's one of a kind animals. Kangaroos are not endangered, but they are one of the continent's best-known animals.

Sydney is Australia's biggest city. The growth of big cities, such as this one, has sometimes pushed Australia's animals out of the places they naturally live.

Australia is also known for the colorful fish that swim in the coral of the Great Barrier Reef.

These Europeans cleared land for homes, roads, and farms. Some of Australia's native animals **adapted** to these changes. Other **species** have become **endangered**. Let's learn more about Australia's endangered animals and how people can help them.

Australia's Climate

Australia has different weather in different places. The kind of weather a place generally has over a long time is called its climate. Australia has a mix of **tropical** climates and **temperate** ones.

The center of Australia is very hot and dry. Most of this part of the continent gets less

Uluru is a rock formation in the middle of Australia. This place has a hot, dry climate.

Australia has a warm, wet climate in the northeast.

Koalas live in forests where there are plenty of eucalyptus trees.

than 10 inches (25 cm) of rain each year. The northern and northeastern parts of Australia get about four times as much rain as the central part. That means those places get 40 inches (100 cm) of rain each year! Southern Australia has hot summers and cool winters.

Habitats in Australia

Australia has many different habitats. There are deserts, such as the Great Sandy and Tanami deserts. The bilby, the thorny devil, and the endangered rufous hare wallaby live in this hot, dry habitat. Australia also has temperate forests and grassy plains. Kangaroos and wombats live in these kinds of habitats.

The thorny devil is a lizard that lives in Australia's deserts.

There are about 30 different kinds of wallabies in Australia. Only a few kinds of wallabies are endangered.

Australia also has rain forest habitats, too. Birds, bugs, spiders, and many other animals make their homes there. Since the 1700s, more than three-quarters of Australia's rain forests have been destroyed. People are working to **protect** the remaining rain forests. This will help save the animals that live in this habitat.

Australia's Endangered Animals

Australia has many incredible animals. The animals on these pages are endangered and could one day become **extinct**.

MAP KEY

- Numbat
- Gouldian Finch
- Corroboree Frog
- Greater Bilby
- Leadbeater's Possum
- Short-Necked Turtle

Gouldian Finch

1. Corroboree Frog

The tiny corroboree frog lives in forests and bogs high up in Australia's mountains. It is Australia's most endangered frog.

2. Gouldian Finch

The colorful Gouldian finch lives in the woodlands and grasslands of Australia. Today there are only 2,500 left in the wild.

3. Greater Bilby

The greater bilby is close to extinction because of fires in its desert habitat and because of habitat loss.

Australia

Leadbeater's Possum

4. Leadbeater's Possum

The Leadbeater's possum lives in the trees in southeastern Australia in Victoria's Central Highlands. Today there are about 5,000 of these possums left.

5. Numbat

Numbats were once plentiful in the southern part of Australia. Now there are only 2,000 left in the wild.

6. Short-Necked Turtle

Short-necked turtles, also called swamp turtles, live in the swamps of Australia's Swan Coastal Plain. There are thought to be only 15 to 25 of these **reptiles** still living in the wild.

Numbat

Numbats are also known as banded anteaters. These small marsupials use their long noses to find termites. They then dig in the soil with their front claws and stick out their long, sticky tongues to eat their food.

Numbats live in open woodlands and make their homes in fallen logs. These logs also give them a place to hide from dogs, cats, hawks, eagles, and snakes.

Some termite mounds rise high above the ground!

Numbats eat up to 20,000 termites a day!

Scientists guess that there are only 2,000 numbats left there. The biggest dangers to numbats are habitat loss and attacks from red foxes, dogs, and cats.

Short-Necked Turtle

The short-necked turtle is Australia's most **critically** endangered reptile. It was put on the endangered-species list in 1970 because there were only 250 turtles. Today there are thought to be fewer than 25!

The short-necked turtle is also known as the western swamp tortoise. Here is a short-necked turtle swimming in a swamp in Australia.

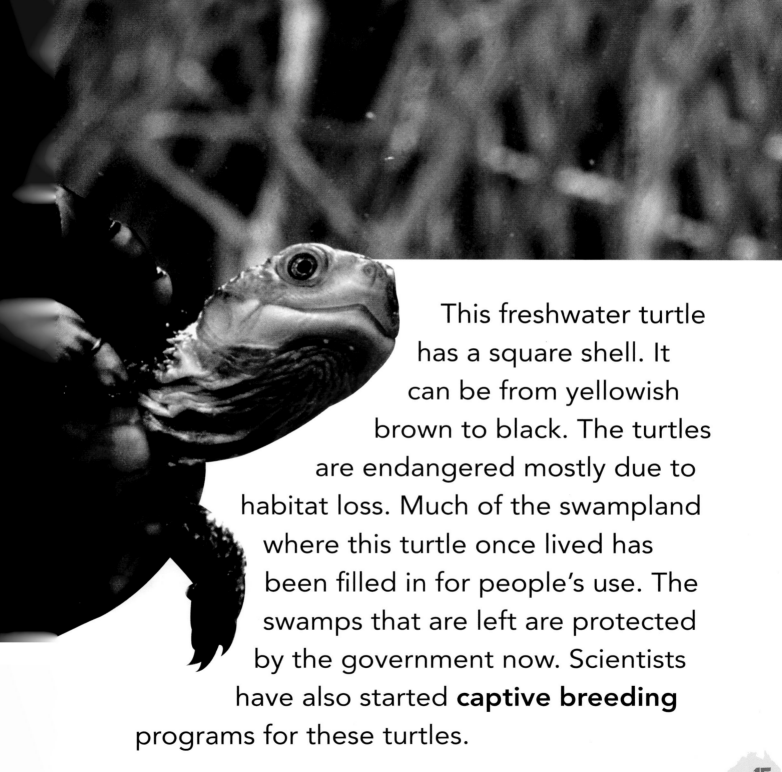

This freshwater turtle has a square shell. It can be from yellowish brown to black. The turtles are endangered mostly due to habitat loss. Much of the swampland where this turtle once lived has been filled in for people's use. The swamps that are left are protected by the government now. Scientists have also started **captive breeding** programs for these turtles.

Northern Hairy-Nosed Wombat

Wombats live in burrows under Australia's dry grassland and woodland habitats. There are three kinds of wombats. These are the common wombat, the southern hairy-nosed wombat, and the northern hairy-nosed wombat. Both of the hairy-nosed wombat species are endangered, but the northern wombats are in the most trouble.

Northern hairy-nosed wombats are critically endangered because of habitat loss and because of competition for food with introduced animals, such as cows, sheep, and rabbits.

Wombats sleep in burrows they dig in the ground.

In 1981, there were fewer than 20 northern hairy-nosed wombats left in Australia. Because of work to protect these animals and their habitat, there are about 113 today. These marsupials are still critically endangered.

Gouldian Finch

Gouldian finches are sometimes called rainbow finches because of their bright coloring. They can have black, green, yellow, and red markings and a purple chest. These finches can have red, black, or yellow heads. Gouldian finches live in tropical, grassy woodlands. They eat mostly grass seeds and they nest in holes in trees. Farm animals, such

This is a male Gouldian finch. You can see why this bird is also called a rainbow finch.

This is a female Gouldian finch. Female Gouldian finches are not as brightly colored as the males are.

as cows and sheep, eat grass before it has a chance to make seeds. This leaves the Gouldian finch without a food supply. People also burn the woodlands to make way for farms, which destroys the finch's habitat.

Giant Clam

Giant clams live in coral reefs in the Phillipines, Micronesia, and Australia. These huge clams can live for 100 years in the wild! They have long been an important food supply for people in these places. People have also been trying to raise giant clams on farms and then let them go in their natural homes. Today, **commercial** fishermen gather those clams, too.

This giant clam lives in Australia's Great Barrier Reef.

Giant clams are the only kind of clam that cannot close its shell all the way.

Giant clams are easy to collect and are now extinct in some places. The number of giant clams has dropped so low in Australia that it is now unlawful to collect them for food there.

Save Australia's Endangered Animals!

There are many reasons animals in Australia have become endangered or extinct. Some have not adapted to the nonnative animals that have been brought to the continent. Others have lost their habitats to farms, businesses, mining, logging, roads, and homes.

Australia's government is working to protect its animals. It has set aside conservation land. The government has captive breeding programs, too. It is also working to teach the people of Australia ways to save native plants and animals.

Glossary

ADAPTED (uh-DAPT-ed) Changed to fit requirements.

CAPTIVE BREEDING (KAP-tiv BREED-ing) Bringing animals together to have babies in a zoo or an aquarium instead of in the wild.

COMMERCIAL (kuh-MER-shul) Having to do with business or trade.

CRITICALLY (KRIH-tih-kuh-lee) Being at a turning point.

ENDANGERED (in-DAYN-jerd) Describing an animal whose species or group has almost all died out.

EXTINCT (ek-STINGKT) No longer existing.

INDIGENOUS (in-DIH-jeh-nus) Having started in and coming naturally from a certain place.

MARSUPIALS (mahr-SOO-pee-ulz) Animals that carry their young in a pouch.

PROTECT (pruh-TEKT) To keep safe.

REPTILES (REP-tylz) Cold-blooded animals with thin, dry pieces of skin called scales.

SPECIES (SPEE-sheez) One kind of living thing. All people are one species.

TEMPERATE (TEM-puh-rut) Not too hot or too cold.

TROPICAL (TRAH-puh-kul) Warm year-round.

Index

Web Sites

Due to the changing nature of Internet links, PowerKids Press has developed an online list of Web sites related to the subject of this book. This site is updated regularly. Please use this link to access the list: www.powerkidslinks.com/sea/aust/